I0530743

Wherever Duty Calls
A Pocket Prayer Guide for Service Members

Title: Wherever Duty Calls
Subtitle: A Pocket Prayer Guide for Service Members

Author: Stephen McGowan
Copyright © 2025 Stephen McGowan

All rights reserved. No part of this book may be reproduced, stored in a retrieval system, or transmitted in any form or by any means—electronic, mechanical, photocopying, recording, or otherwise—without the prior written permission of the publisher, except in the case of brief quotations embodied in critical articles or reviews.

Published by:
Parapet Books
Brooklyn, NY
www.parapetbooks.com

Interior Design and Formatting: Parapet Books
First Edition: May 2025
ISBN: 979-8-9990832-3-4

This is a work of fiction. Names, characters, places, and incidents either are the product of the author's imagination or are used fictitiously. Any resemblance to actual persons, living or dead, events, or locales is entirely coincidental.

For information about bulk purchases, special editions, or rights inquiries, please contact:
info@parapetbooks.com

Printed in the United States of America

Wherever Duty Calls

A Pocket Prayer Guide for Service Members

PARAPET BOOKS

Table of Contents

Introduction

To my brothers and sisters in uniform

Even if this is your very first day in the military, you already know this life isn't easy. I've been doing it for over twenty years now, and I can tell you: there's nothing else quite like it. I've been pushed past what I thought were my limits, I've felt pride and heartbreak all in the same day, and I've stood shoulder to shoulder with some of the finest people I'll ever know.

And yet — with everything I've done and seen — one thing has always been hard for me: praying.

I haven't always had the right words. I haven't always felt religious enough. Sometimes the only prayer I could manage was just a quiet thought whispered to myself.

I'll never forget one mission in Afghanistan. We were supposed to be out for a day — but by day four, I was lying in a farmer's field in a makeshift patrol base, hungry, tired, and listening to reports that the Taliban were closing in on us. I stared up at the sky that night wanting so badly to pray — to say something to God — but I just didn't know how to start. So I did the only thing I could think of: I turned to my battle buddy and asked, *"Hey man… will you pray for me?"*

He did. Right there in that dirt field, surrounded by all the unknowns, a simple prayer brought me a peace I still can't quite explain.

From that day on, I started paying closer attention to prayers — the ones I heard from chaplains, the ones my buddies whispered before a mission, the ones I scribbled in a notebook so I wouldn't forget. Over time, I realized these simple words were like armor for my mind and hope for my heart.

That's why I made this book. It's not fancy. It's not complicated. It's a pocketful of honest prayers and powerful Bible verses for real people serving in a real world that can be tough and beautiful all at once.

Keep this guide with you — in a pocket, a rucksack, a cargo pocket, or tucked in next to your

Bible. Pull it out when you're standing in line at chow, when you're exhausted at the end of a long day, when you're lying in your bunk missing home, or when you just don't know what to say to God.

If you're like me and sometimes prayer feels awkward or hard — I hope these words help you talk to the one who knows your heart better than you do. May this little book remind you that no matter where you go, you never walk alone.

Thank you for what you do. Thank you for standing the watch, carrying the load, and looking out for the rest of us. May the Lord bless you, protect you, and give you courage for every battle ahead — inside and out.

Stay strong. Stay faithful. And never stop growing.

How to Use This Book

T his little book was never meant to sit on a shelf. It's meant to be stuffed in a cargo pocket, tucked under your pillow, slipped into your ruck, or kept on your desk where you can grab it fast.

You don't have to read it front to back. Flip through it however you need:

- **When you're waking up early for PT**, open to the *Daily Prayers for Strength and Courage*.
- **When you're far from home and missing your people**, go to *Prayers for Homesickness and Loneliness*.
- **When fear creeps in and you feel the weight of danger**, find *Prayers for Times of Fear and Danger*.

- **When you need help to do what's right**, read *Prayers for Moral Strength and Integrity*.
- **When your family is heavy on your heart**, turn to *Prayers for Strength for Family and Loved Ones*.
- **When you don't know what to say at all**, flip to the *Favorite Verses for Quick Reference* — sometimes one line of scripture says more than a thousand words.

This is not a book of perfect, polished prayers — these are real words for real people in real situations. Use them as a starting point. Whisper them as they are, or change them into your own words. God doesn't need fancy language — He just wants to hear your heart.

Share it if you want to. If a battle buddy is struggling, hand it over for a while. Mark your favorite pages, jot notes in the margins, circle verses that mean the most to you. Make it yours.

Above all, remember: prayer isn't about saying it perfectly — it's about remembering you're never alone. You've got a God who walks every patrol, stands every watch, and sits beside you in the dark moments when no one else can.

May this book help you find courage, peace, and a steady heart, wherever you serve.

Stay strong. Keep the faith. See you on the high ground.

Daily Prayers for Strength and Courage

Quick Verses for Daily Strength

- *"I can do all things through Christ who strengthens me."* — Philippians 4:13
- *"The Lord is my light and my salvation—whom shall I fear?"* — Psalm 27:1

Morning Prayer Before PT

Prayer:
Heavenly Father, as I rise to face this day, I ask for Your strength to carry me through every task ahead. Give me courage when I am afraid, discipline when I am weary, and wisdom in every choice I make. Walk beside me and guard my steps. In Jesus' name, Amen.

Scripture:
"Have I not commanded you? Be strong and courageous. Do not be afraid; do not be discouraged, for the Lord your God will be with you wherever you go."
— Joshua 1:9

Prayer for Courage in Fearful Moments

Prayer:
Lord, when fear grips my heart and danger surrounds me, remind me that You are greater than anything I face. Fill me with courage that comes only from You. Help me stand firm and trust that You fight for me. Amen.

Scripture:
"So do not fear, for I am with you; do not be dismayed, for I am your God. I will strengthen you and help you; I will uphold you with my righteous right hand."
— Isaiah 41:10

Evening Prayer for Rest

Prayer:
Father, thank You for staying with me through this day. Take my worries and fears tonight. Grant me deep rest and renew my strength for tomorrow. Watch over my loved ones and bring peace to my heart. Amen.

Scripture:
"Come to me, all you who are weary and burdened, and I will give you rest."
— Matthew 11:28

Prayers for Basic Training or Hard Training Exercises

Quick Verses for Hard Days

- *"I press on toward the goal to win the prize for which God has called me heavenward in Christ Jesus."* — Philippians 3:14
- *"Be strong and take heart, all you who hope in the Lord."* — Psalm 31:24

Prayer for Perseverance

Prayer:
Lord, some days feel too hard and my body is worn out. Give me endurance to push through every obstacle. Remind me that with You, I can persevere and finish strong. Make my mind steady and my spirit willing. Amen.

Scripture:
"Let us run with perseverance the race marked out for us, fixing our eyes on Jesus, the pioneer and perfecter of faith."
— Hebrews 12:1-2

Prayer for Discipline and Focus

Prayer:
Father, help me stay focused and disciplined in my training and duties. Keep my thoughts clear and my actions honorable. Teach me to serve with integrity and give my best, even when no one is watching. Amen.

Scripture:
"No discipline seems pleasant at the time, but painful. Later on, however, it produces a harvest of righteousness and peace for those who have been trained by it."
— Hebrews 12:11

Prayer for Endurance When Exhausted

Prayer:
God, when I feel completely spent, strengthen my body and renew my spirit. Help me take one more step, run one more mile, complete one more task. Be my energy when I have none left. Thank You for never leaving my side. Amen.

Scripture:
"But those who hope in the Lord will renew their strength. They will soar on wings like eagles; they will run and not grow weary, they will walk and not be faint."
— Isaiah 40:31

Prayers for Deployment and Separation from Loved Ones

Quick Verses for Deployment

- *"I am with you always, to the very end of the age."* — Matthew 28:20
- *"The Lord will fight for you; you need only to be still."* — Exodus 14:14

Prayer for Protection Far from Home

Prayer:
Lord, as I serve far from my home and family, I ask for Your hand of protection over me. Guard my life, my heart, and my mind. Keep me alert and safe in every situation. May Your presence be my constant shelter. Amen.

Scripture:
"Whoever dwells in the shelter of the Most High will rest in the shadow of the Almighty."
— Psalm 91:1

Prayer for Family Back Home

Prayer:
Father, watch over those I love while I am away. Protect them, provide for them, and fill their days with peace. Calm their worries and remind them that You love them even more than I do. Bring us back together in Your perfect timing. Amen.

Scripture:
"Peace I leave with you; my peace I give you. I do not give

to you as the world gives. Do not let your hearts be troubled and do not be afraid."
— John 14:27

Prayer for Hope and Reunion

Prayer:
God of hope, help me hold onto the promise that we will be together again soon. When I feel the ache of distance, remind me that You are near and nothing can separate me from Your love. Give me hope that steadies my heart until I return home. Amen.

Scripture:
"The Lord will watch over your coming and going both now and forevermore."
— Psalm 121:8

Prayers for Times of Fear and Danger

Quick Verses for Courage

- *"When I am afraid, I put my trust in You."* — Psalm 56:3
- *"The Lord is my strength and my shield; my heart trusts in Him, and He helps me."* — Psalm 28:7
- *"No weapon forged against you will prevail."* — Isaiah 54:17

Prayer for Calm in Combat or Threat

Prayer:

Lord, when I face danger, steady my hands and calm my heart. Remove fear and replace it with clear mind and courage. Protect me and my brothers and sisters beside me. Help me trust that You are my shield in every battle. Amen.

Scripture:

"Even though I walk through the darkest valley, I will fear no evil, for You are with me; Your rod and Your staff, they comfort me."
— Psalm 23:4

Prayer for Peace When Fear Overwhelms

Prayer:

God, when fear grips my chest and I can't see the way forward, remind me You are near. Breathe Your peace into my soul and quiet every anxious thought. Make me strong and courageous because I know You hold my life in Your hands. Amen.

Scripture:
"The Lord is my light and my salvation — whom shall I fear? The Lord is the stronghold of my life — of whom shall I be afraid?"
— Psalm 27:1

Prayer for Courage Under Fire

Prayer:
Heavenly Father, in moments of chaos and danger, make me brave. Help me think clearly, act wisely, and protect those around me. Let me lean on Your promise that You go before me and fight for me. Amen.

Scripture:
"Be strong and courageous. Do not be afraid or terrified because of them, for the Lord your God goes with you; He will never leave you nor forsake you."
— Deuteronomy 31:6

Prayer When Feeling Alone in Danger

Prayer:
Lord, when I feel surrounded and alone, remind me I am never truly alone. You are my Defender and Deliverer. Stand guard over me and fill my heart with unshakable trust in You. Amen.

Scripture:
"The angel of the Lord encamps around those who fear Him, and He delivers them."
— Psalm 34:7

Prayers for Comrades and Unit

Quick Verses for Brotherhood

- *"How good and pleasant it is when God's people live together in unity!"* — Psalm 133:1
- *"Carry each other's burdens, and in this way you will fulfill the law of Christ."* — Galatians 6:2
- *"Be devoted to one another in love. Honor one another above yourselves."* — Romans 12:10

Prayer for Unity and Brotherhood

Prayer:
Lord, thank You for the brothers and sisters I serve beside each day. Bind us together in trust and loyalty. Help us look out for one another and work as one body. May our teamwork be strong and our bond unbreakable. Amen.

Scripture:
"Though one may be overpowered, two can defend themselves. A cord of three strands is not quickly broken."
— Ecclesiastes 4:12

Prayer for Leadership and Wise Decisions

Prayer:
God, grant our leaders wisdom and courage to make good decisions. Guide them with Your truth and protect them from pride and fear. Help me support my leaders and show respect, so that our unit stays strong and ready. Amen.

Scripture:
"If any of you lacks wisdom, you should ask God, who gives generously to all without finding fault, and it will be given to you."
— James 1:5

Prayer for a Fallen Comrade

Prayer:
Lord, today I remember those who have laid down their lives for others. Comfort the families who mourn. Give me strength to honor their sacrifice through how I live and serve. May their memory remind us of the price of freedom and the hope of eternal life in You. Amen.

Scripture:
"Greater love has no one than this: to lay down one's life for one's friends."
— John 15:13

Prayer for Safety of My Unit

Prayer:
Heavenly Father, watch over my unit as we train, travel, and deploy. Surround us with Your angels and protect us from harm and hidden dangers. Bring each one of us safely home when our work is done. Amen.

Scripture:
"The Lord will keep you from all harm — He will watch over your life."
— Psalm 121:7

Prayer for Peace and Good Morale

Prayer:
Lord, in the stress of long days and hard missions, fill our hearts with peace. Keep our spirits strong and our attitudes positive. Help us encourage each other and lift each other up when morale is low. Amen.

Scripture:
"Therefore encourage one another and build each other up, just as in fact you are doing."
— 1 Thessalonians 5:11

Prayers for Homesickness and Loneliness

Quick Verses for Homesickness

- *"I will not leave you as orphans; I will come to you."* — John 14:18
- *"My presence will go with you, and I will give you rest."* — Exodus 33:14
- *"The Lord is my shepherd; I lack nothing."* — Psalm 23:1

Prayer for Comfort When Missing Home

Prayer:
Lord, You know how much I miss my family, my friends, and the comfort of home. Fill the empty places in my heart with Your presence. Help me remember that no distance can separate me from Your love or from the love of those who wait for me. Amen.

Scripture:
"The Lord is close to the brokenhearted and saves those who are crushed in spirit."
— Psalm 34:18

Prayer for Connection with Others

Prayer:
God, when loneliness creeps in, open my eyes to the people around me. Help me build true friendships and find community, even far from home. Remind me that You created us to stand together, not alone. Amen.

Scripture:
"Carry each other's burdens, and in this way you will fulfill the law of Christ."
— Galatians 6:2

Prayer for Nights When I Feel Alone

Prayer:
Father, the nights can feel long and heavy when I'm away from home. Quiet my mind and ease my longing for loved ones. Remind me that You watch over me as I sleep and that You hold those I love close to Your heart, too. Amen.

Scripture:
"In peace I will lie down and sleep, for You alone, Lord, make me dwell in safety."
— Psalm 4:8

Prayer for Trusting God's Timing

Prayer:
Lord, when the days feel endless and the wait to

go home seems too long, give me patience and trust in Your perfect timing. Teach me to make the most of where I am and to trust that You will reunite me with my loved ones in Your good plan. Amen.

Scripture:
"Trust in the Lord with all your heart and lean not on your own understanding; in all your ways submit to Him, and He will make your paths straight."
— Proverbs 3:5-6

Prayer for Hope in Loneliness

Prayer:
God, remind me that I am never truly alone. Fill my lonely moments with Your hope and remind me of all the people praying for me back home. Strengthen my heart to keep going with courage and faith. Amen.

Scripture:
"Never will I leave you; never will I forsake you."
— Hebrews 13:5

Prayers for Moral Strength and Integrity

Quick Verses for Moral Strength

- *"Blessed are those whose ways are blameless, who walk according to the law of the Lord."* — Psalm 119:1
- *"Let your light shine before others, that they may see your good deeds and glorify your Father in heaven."* — Matthew 5:16
- *"Above all else, guard your heart, for everything you do flows from it."* — Proverbs 4:23

Prayer to Stand Firm in Temptation

Prayer:
Lord, help me stand strong when I'm tempted to do what I know is wrong. Remind me who I am and who I belong to. Give me the courage to walk away from anything that dishonors You, even when no one else is watching. Amen.

Scripture:
"No temptation has overtaken you except what is common to mankind. And God is faithful; He will not let you be tempted beyond what you can bear."
— 1 Corinthians 10:13

Prayer for Integrity on and off Duty

Prayer:
God, help me live with integrity — not just when people are looking, but when it's just me and You. Make my words honest and my actions right. Give me the strength to do the hard but honorable thing, every time. Amen.

Scripture:
"The integrity of the upright guides them, but the unfaithful are destroyed by their duplicity."
— Proverbs 11:3

Prayer for Wisdom in Hard Choices

Prayer:
Father, sometimes the right choice isn't clear or easy. Give me wisdom to know what is true, and courage to do what is right, even if it costs me something. Guide my steps so that my life points others back to You. Amen.

Scripture:
"If any of you lacks wisdom, you should ask God, who gives generously to all without finding fault, and it will be given to you."
— James 1:5

Prayer for Strength Against Peer Pressure

Prayer:
Lord, help me not to follow the crowd when they go the wrong way. Give me the backbone to stand alone if I have to. Surround me with friends who help me stay true and push me to be better every day. Amen.

Scripture:
"Do not be misled: 'Bad company corrupts good character.'"
— 1 Corinthians 15:33

Prayer for Daily Renewal of Heart

Prayer:
God, search my heart and clean out anything that doesn't honor You. Make me new each day. When I mess up, help me run back to You quickly and start again. Thank You for never giving up on me. Amen.

Scripture:
"Create in me a pure heart, O God, and renew a steadfast spirit within me."
— Psalm 51:10

Prayers for Strength for Family and Loved Ones

Quick Verses for Family Strength

- *"As for me and my household, we will serve the Lord."* — Joshua 24:15
- *"Be devoted to one another in love. Honor one another above yourselves."* — Romans 12:10
- *"Love bears all things, believes all things, hopes all things, endures all things."* — 1 Corinthians 13:7

Prayer for My Spouse or Partner

Prayer:
Lord, thank You for the one I love back home. Strengthen them while we are apart. Give them patience for the long days, peace for the lonely nights, and courage to face whatever comes their way. Help them feel how much they are loved — by me, and even more by You. Amen.

Scripture:
"The Lord bless you and keep you; the Lord make His face shine on you and be gracious to you."
— Numbers 6:24-25

Prayer for My Children

Prayer:
Father, watch over my kids while I'm away. Protect their hearts and minds. Surround them with good people who will love them and teach them well. Help them know I think of them every single day, and remind them that You are always with them. Amen.

Scripture:
"All your children will be taught by the Lord, and great will be their peace."
— Isaiah 54:13

Prayer for Parents and Family Back Home

Prayer:
God, thank You for the family who raised me and loves me still. Take care of them while I'm far away. Keep them healthy, provide for their needs, and fill their homes with peace. Remind them that You are holding us all close, no matter the miles between us. Amen.

Scripture:
"Honor your father and your mother, so that you may live long in the land the Lord your God is giving you."
— Exodus 20:12

Prayer for Loved Ones' Worries

Prayer:
Lord, I know my loved ones worry about me. Calm their fears. Give them trust that I am in Your hands. Replace their anxiety with faith and their sleepless nights with rest. Fill their hearts with hope until we're together again. Amen.

Scripture:
"Cast all your anxiety on Him because He cares for you."
— 1 Peter 5:7

Prayer for Reunion and Restoration

Prayer:
Father, I look forward to the day when this time apart is over. Prepare our hearts for a joyful reunion. Heal any strain caused by distance. Bring us back together stronger than ever, full of gratitude for every moment we have. Amen.

Scripture:
"The Lord will watch over your coming and going both now and forevermore."
— Psalm 121:8

Favorite Verses for Quick Reference

These verses have brought me peace, courage, and hope more times than I can count. When you need to steady your heart in a hurry, flip here — whisper one of these out loud or keep it in your mind until the storm passes.

Verses for Courage

- *"Be strong and courageous. Do not be afraid or discouraged, for the Lord your God will be with you wherever you go."*
  — Joshua 1:9
- *"The Lord is my light and my salvation — whom shall I fear? The Lord is the stronghold of my life — of whom shall I be afraid?"*
  — Psalm 27:1
- *"When I am afraid, I put my trust in You."*
  — Psalm 56:3

Verses for Strength

- *"I can do all things through Christ who gives me strength."*
  — Philippians 4:13

- *"God is our refuge and strength, an ever-present help in trouble."*
  — Psalm 46:1
- *"The Lord is my strength and my shield; my heart trusts in Him, and He helps me."*
  — Psalm 28:7

Verses for Peace

- *"Peace I leave with you; my peace I give you. I do not give to you as the world gives. Do not let your hearts be troubled and do not be afraid."*
  — John 14:27
- *"Cast all your anxiety on Him because He cares for you."*
  — 1 Peter 5:7
- *"In peace I will lie down and sleep, for You alone, Lord, make me dwell in safety."*
  — Psalm 4:8

Verses for Hope

- *"For I know the plans I have for you,"*
  declares the Lord, "plans to prosper you
  and not to harm you, plans to give you hope
  and a future."
  — Jeremiah 29:11
- *"The Lord your God is with you, the*
  Mighty Warrior who saves."
  — Zephaniah 3:17
- *"Let us hold unswervingly to the hope we*
  profess, for He who promised is faithful."
  — Hebrews 10:23

Verses for Protection

- *"The Lord will fight for you; you need only*
  to be still."
  — Exodus 14:14
- *"The angel of the Lord encamps around*
  those who fear Him, and He delivers
  them."
  — Psalm 34:7

- *"No weapon forged against you will prevail."*
  — Isaiah 54:17

Verses for Daily Encouragement

- *"Trust in the Lord with all your heart and lean not on your own understanding."*
  — Proverbs 3:5
- *"The Lord bless you and keep you; the Lord make His face shine on you and be gracious to you."*
  — Numbers 6:24-25
- *"Surely goodness and mercy shall follow me all the days of my life."*
  — Psalm 23:6

A Closing Word from Me

To everyone who holds this little book —

If you've read this far, I want to thank you for letting me share a piece of my own journey with you. I've walked this road in uniform for over twenty years now. I've faced days I thought I wouldn't make it through, and days I wished would never end. Through it all, my faith, these prayers, and the people standing beside me have carried me farther than I ever could have gone alone.

I know what it's like to feel far from home, far from comfort, and sometimes far from hope. My prayer is that when you find yourself in those places, this pocket guide reminds you that you're never really alone. You are part of a brotherhood and sisterhood that stretches across time and continents — and you're loved by a God who stands watch even when you sleep.

May these words give you strength when you feel weak, courage when fear creeps in, and hope when the road feels long. And when you don't

know what to pray, just start with anything —
He's always listening.

Thank you for your service. Thank you for your
sacrifice. Keep your head up, your heart strong,
and your mind focused on what matters most.

See you on the high ground.

— Stephen McGowan
Proud to stand beside you.

www.ingramcontent.com/pod-product-compliance
Lightning Source LLC
Chambersburg PA
CBHW011225120626
46545CB00010B/3164

* 9 7 9 8 9 9 9 0 8 3 2 3 4 *